Alluvial

Alluvial
MY PHOTOGRAPHIC JOURNAL OF THE LOWER MISSISSIPPI RIVER VALLEY
Randy P. Roussel

Dévoué à tous ces disposés pour faire le voyage.

296 of 500

First Edition

Contents

INTRODUCTION

Alluvial Places

I have always lived upon the alluvium created by the Mississippi River. I know the taste of the sweet sugar cane that grows in its fertile soil. I sit on the levee that protects the land and wonder where the ships and barges plying the River have been; where they are going. The River's powerful currents and annual floods dictate life along its banks. The humid breezes from the River create a temperate climate. The Father of Waters is the origin of the life I know.

What follows is not a documentary of this vast area. Rather, it is a sharing of favorite places. I hope you may appreciate these places as much as I do.

Acknowledgments

I would like to thank my wife, Darrelyn, and my children, Randi, Ryann, and Jason, for their support of this project. I would also like to thank Stephanie Riegel for her insightful critique of the stories and Paola Gianturco for her time in reviewing the text and photographs. Finally, I would like to thank Dan Pratt and Jim Pratt for their commitment to my projects.

The Mississippi

The Mississippi River will always have its own way.

MARK TWAIN

The Mississippi River begins at Lake Itasca in Minnesota and flows for approximately 2,320 miles to the Gulf of Mexico. It serves as the drainage basin of most of everything between the Eastern and Western Continental Divides. At Lake Itasca, it would take the River ten minutes to fill one semi-trailer with water. At New Orleans, 166 semi-trailers of water flow past Algiers Point each second. This number is multiplied during flood stage.

Given its way, the Mississippi River would change course. It would bypass New Orleans and flow through the Atchafalaya Basin, one of its historical routes to the Gulf. Because the Corps of Engineers, politics, and other manmade forces refuse to let this happen, the River continues to flow through Baton Rouge and New Orleans, eventually winding its way to the Gulf.

The River and the people along its banks are not only the inspiration for my stories but also have served to inspire stories by Mark Twain and Francis Parkinson Keyes, as well as the songs of Memphis Minnie. The River was my front yard growing up. The River is the view from my office. The River is my past, my present, and my future.

The Atchafalaya Basin

I enter a swamp as a sacred place, a sanctum sanctorum.

HENRY DAVID THOREAU, *WALDEN*

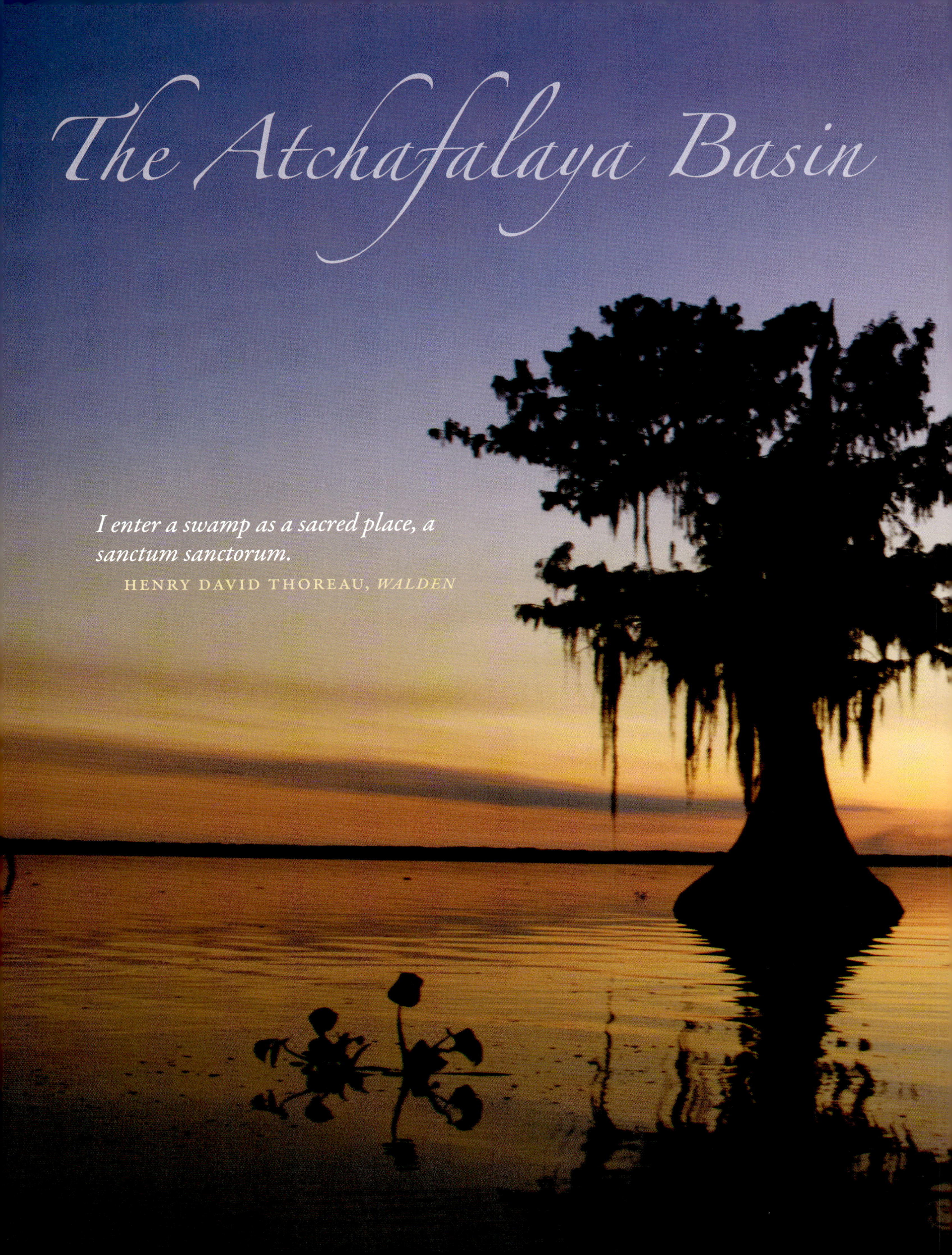

I am fascinated with the circuitous path the Mississippi River has taken over history. The path was not created by water cutting through rock, but by water forcing its way through the fine-grained soil it carries, creating land in the process. The River's main channel has been the Atchafalaya Basin, the bayous of Lafourche and Terrebonne Parishes, and the route we know today. The Atchafalaya Basin was formed by this precarious process of the alluvial waters creating land and the Gulf of Mexico taking it back, with the River changing its course, only to return.

I appreciate each visit to the Atchafalaya Basin, as each sunrise and sunset is unique. The Atchafalaya on a foggy morning, when I am unable to see but a few feet before me, is not the same place as when a strong north wind clears the sky. Natural conditions, over which I have no control, dictate the everchanging palate I see. An abundance of wildlife, both pleasant and hostile, inhabit this area. The Atchafalaya is a combination of open water, shallow streams, and marsh unable to support more than a few pounds of weight. It is a place of discovery and adventure.

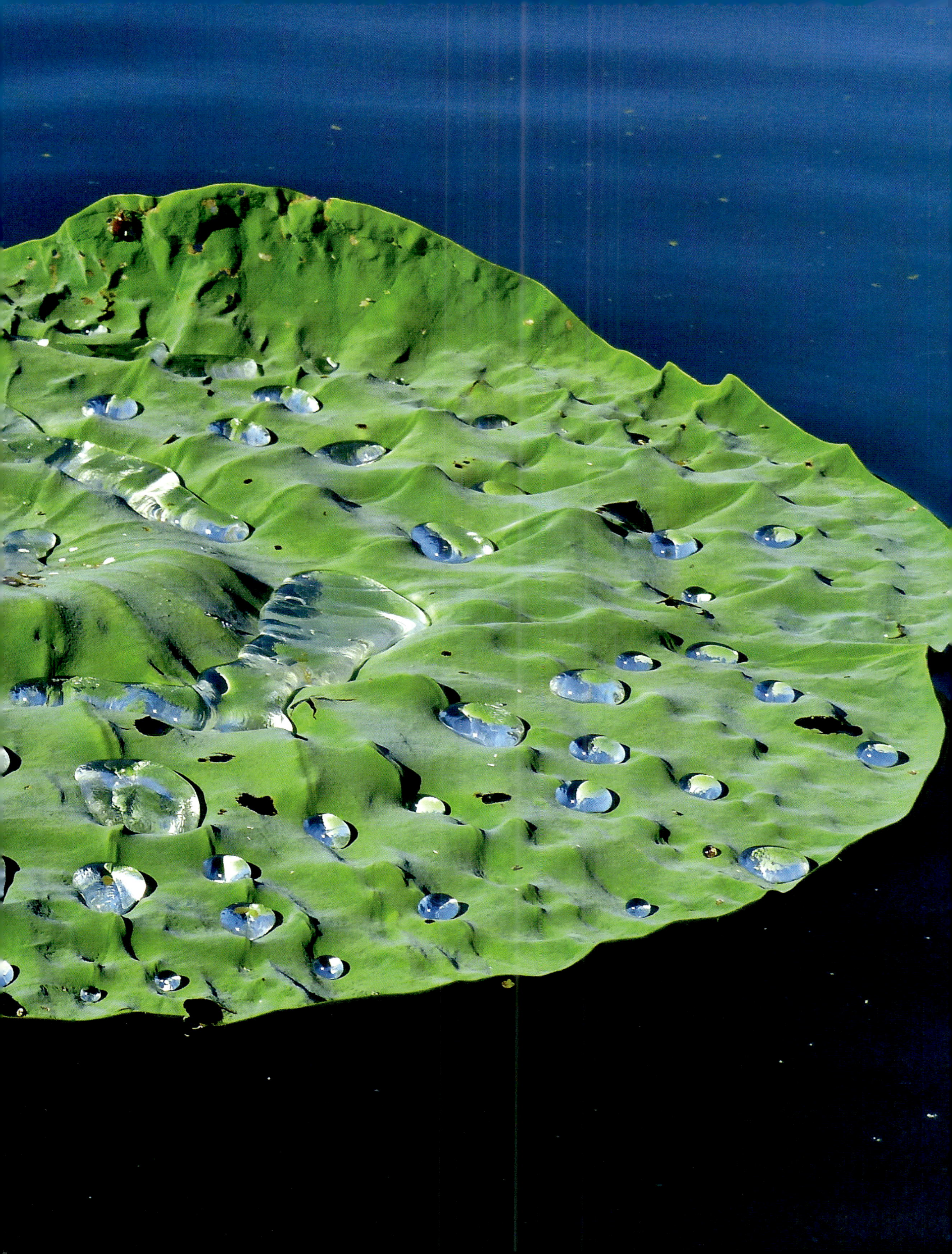

The LSU Lakes

A lake carries you into recesses of feeling otherwise impenetrable.

WILLIAM WORDSWORTH

In 1933, four separate donors gave Louisiana State University the tupelo cypress swamp next to its current campus with the stipulation that the swamp be transformed into lakes and parks for public use. LSU, with the help of the Depression-era WPA, created a gem of seven interconnected lakes. It is public space with abundant wildlife.

I look forward to my visits to University, City Park, and the other lakes. I enjoy the unplanned visits with friends who spontaneously join me for a bike ride. I have come to know others, not by their names but by their gaits. The varying climate makes each day unique, whether it is a misty morning or an evening with the burning sun dropping below the horizon. I pause to glance at the works on the easels of the artists capturing the beauty of the lakes. I go past photographers with their cameras clicking away. I know one photographer who spends every afternoon at the lakes when the white pelicans arrive. She never tires in the pursuit of capturing the perfect moment. I suspect poets are among the fortunate ones inspired by the lakes, even if their poetry never leaves their living rooms.

The Campanile

Where stately oaks and broad magnolias shade inspiring halls.

LSU ALMA MATER

The Campanile is the 175-foot clock tower in the center of Louisiana State University. It was erected in 1923 as a memorial to those from Louisiana who died in World War I—the war to end all wars.

The Campanile plays the Westminster Chimes every quarter hour, with four additional chimes sounding at each quarter hour. On the hour, you hear the full sixteen notes, followed by the tolling of the bell to indicate the hour. At noon, the alma mater is played. My undergraduate classes were in the buildings called the quad, located next to the Campanile. I would count the increased succession of chimes, leading to the anticipation of the lecture ending and my eventual chance to relax under the adjoining oak trees.

The Campanile, visible from every point, is the landmark for navigation around the campus. The Parade Grounds front the Campanile on its side opposite from the quad. The Parade Grounds are the perfect tailgate location before football games. Here, we can throw the perfect pass after eating jambalaya. It is where the frisbee players compete in their sport. It is where dogs and kids run free.

Maybe it is the flags at the tower, either sailing in the wind or flat against the flagpole on a windless day. Maybe it is the way the moon plays hide and seek with the tower. Maybe it is because of my memory of the chimes serving as an alarm clock, letting me know class was over. Maybe it is the way the tower foretells of a coming storm, but for reasons I cannot precisely identify, each visit to the Campanile evokes a different feeling.

Trees

Trees are poems the earth
writes upon the sky.

KAHIL GIBRAN

The cypress tree is the image of Louisiana to many, but an oak tree is my true love. An oak tree has a long life, with its beauty and purpose improving with age. I would like to think it will be the same with me.

The land along the River Road is filled with an endless succession of expansive oak trees. Some oaks form an alley to a house; others provide respite from the summer heat. Many times I see a lone oak in a wide flat place, its enduring branches reaching to the sky. I see its isolated beauty; I see its lonely existence. I cannot help but to take time to admire a magnificent oak.

When the Spanish moss on the oak trees trap the sun's rays, it appears as though the oaks are adorned with jewelry. Oak trees also provide recreation. I remember that as a child I would climb their sweeping branches forming perfect ladders to the top of the tree. I would sit on the wide upper branches, rest my back against the main trunk, and enjoy an unobstructed view of the landscape.

Manresa

Silence more musical than any song.

CHRISTINA ROSSETTI

The College of Jefferson was chartered in 1831 and became St. Mary's Jefferson College in 1864. Except when occupied by Union troops during the Civil War, it served as the major educational institution for sons of planters along the River. The Jesuits purchased the college in 1931, converting the property from a college to the "Manresa House of Retreats." In the 1970s the main building at Manresa was slated for demolition, to be replaced by modern buildings. Fortunately, opposition to the proposal triumphed, preserving this historical treasure.

The beauty of Manresa surpasses my ability to capture it in photographs. The silence under the arms of the oaks must be felt to be understood. It cannot be seen. The sun brightens the white-washed walls and casts exotic shadows every morning and evening. The evening breeze on the broad veranda brings repose.

The purpose of a religious retreat at Manresa is to contemplate God's message in silence, guided by skilled theologians. In this serene setting, I come to feel God's presence, and understand that it is not material possessions but my connection to faith and nature that sustains me.

The Hunt

There is a passion for hunting something deeply implanted in the human breast.

CHARLES DICKENS, *OLIVER TWIST*

It is not the hunt, but comradery enjoyed with those I hunt with, that make it a special occasion. It is the shared experience of rising before dawn, enjoying the sunrise from the marsh. It is the hot coffee in the blind and the vigilant search of the sky. After a successful hunt, I return to the camp and have the rare opportunity to take a nap, sip an afternoon Old Fashioned, perhaps smoke a cigar, and enjoy gumbo for supper. The meal is followed by tall tales and games of bourre. One camp to which I am invited is accessible only by boat. Other camps I have visited are not as remote. But all offer a version of a day of friendship and a connection to the outdoors.

I did not duck hunt until I was an adult. My dad considered crawfishing and trapping crabs more enjoyable. When crawfishing with Dad, my sister, and my brothers, I was not stationary as when I am in a blind, but rather I was constantly moving, wading through knee-deep water, using a long pole to lift the nets hopefully filled with crawfish feasting on the bait. I would carefully watch the water for the snakes I frequently came across when wading through the water. I realize the experience of the hunt is not the prey or the location, but the opportunity to connect to nature and to be with friends and family.

Rhythm

The city makes a rhythmic sound that inspires.

RANDI GIDDINGS

The musical legacy developed along the lower Mississippi River is profound. It is jazz, gospel, the blues, all evolving into rock 'n roll. It is the words and melody of "What a Wonderful World" from Louis Armstrong; it is the sound of Irma Thomas.

While jazz is based in African and Caribbean musical techniques and traditions, it was also influenced by the French, Germans, and Italians. Jazz heavily relies on European instruments such as the trumpet, clarinet, and the saxophone. Jazz is America's truly original art form. The numerous and diverse cultures rooted in New Orleans came together to create this unique form of music.

True jazz is similar to life. Jazz is improvisation, with each instrument playing a solo performance supported by a rhythm section playing chords that outline the structure. Each jazz performer interprets a tune in an individual way, never playing the same composition twice. The same is true in life. I am influenced by those around me, but at the same time I speak with my own voice.

I have not decided if listening to blues and jazz is but a form of self-medication. I hear the music and words of lost love. I hear the pains endured. I hear the human experience.

The street performers, bars, and clubs fill the New Orleans air with sounds rooted in jazz and the blues. As I wander around to listen, I realize that I am not witnessing the tomorrow promised yesterday, but the reality of today.

SOUTHERN

French Quarter

New Orleans is a comfortable metropolis which has a certain apathy and stagnation which I find inoffensive.

JOHN KENNEDY TOOLE, *A CONFEDERACY OF DUNCES*

Place d'Armes is the original name of the main square in New Orleans and is located in the French Quarter. The Baroness Pontalba had it renamed Jackson Square in honor of Andrew Jackson, the hero of the Battle of New Orleans. The Baroness commissioned Jackson's bronze statue in the center of the square. Rumor has it that Andrew Jackson would not tip his hat at the Baroness (a gesture of respect) because she frequently wore pants. True to her character, the bronze statue she commissioned portrays Jackson tipping his hat towards her residence at 5 St. Peters.

The square is bordered on its upriver and downriver sides by the Upper and Lower Pontalba Apartment buildings. The River forms the third border. Opposite the River is St. Louis Cathedral, the Cabildo, and the Presbytere. The ironwork adorning the lower steeples of the Cathedral have Adinkra symbols that roughly translate to "asase ye duru" (the Earth has weight) and "sankofa" (the future is dependent on past wisdom), placed there by enslaved West African ironworkers.

Built in 1850, the Pontalba Apartments were home to William Faulker, Edna St. Vincent Millay, Sherwood Anderson, and many others. The Pontalba Apartments inspired stories by Truman Capote, a New Orleans native. I frequently visit an apartment on St. Ann Street in the Lower Pontalba building. The staircase at St. Ann is my entry to a sanctuary from the madding crowds of the French Quarter. I watch people from the apartment balcony overlooking the square. I see individuals that run the gamut of humanity. I see the nicely dressed tourist, the party-goers, the musicians, and the mimes. I see the artists, lining their wares along the wrought-iron fence that encloses the square. The sensory stimulation inspires me to understand more than the mundane.

Dauphine
ONE WAY

JOE'S
FRENCH QUARTER
WINE CELLAR
WINES-LIQUORS
BEER-CHAMPAGNES
Rue St. Pierre
St. Peter

2018
2016

Camp
FedEx

End of the Day

In dreams begins responsibility.

W. B. YEATS

The cane fields were burning—part of the annual ritual of burning the fields before the harvest.

I enjoyed the day. One with no agenda, just discovery on Lake Fausse. A day to renew my mind and spirit.

I spent the day exploring the lake's nooks and crannies. As the sun dropped low in the horizon and a gentle breeze came across the lake, I knew nature's alarm clock had sounded.

I looked over my shoulder, past the motor of the boat, to contemplate the adventure. The array of colors in the sky were reflected in the waters.

And I enjoyed that special moment in time at the End of the Day.

The End of the Day is not unique to me. It is something we all experience.

The End of the Day means pursuing our passions, bonding with friends and family. It means loving something that can be touched by death.

The End of the Day is not a physical place; it is an emotional one. It is the glance at the sunset, whether from Lake Fausse or the porch.

The End of the Day is the moment of reflection to think about who we are.

You could tell from the way he talked, though, he had gone to school a long time. That was probably what was wrong with him.

JOHN KENNEDY TOOLE, *A CONFEDERACY OF DUNCES*

i

x

6

ii

xii

8

vi

2

10

viii

4

12

14

15

16

18

20

To me, seeing a caption on a photograph is like seeing a scratch on a smooth surface. So with that in mind, I've placed the captions below instead:

p. i Lake Martin, near Breaux Bridge, Louisiana

p. ii Lake Fausse Pointe State Park, near Morgan City, Louisiana

p. vi University Lake, Baton Rouge

p. viii Lake Fausse, near Morgan City, Louisiana

p. x Lake Fausse, near Morgan City, Louisiana

p. xii View of the Mississippi River from Baton Rouge

p. 2 View of the Mississippi River at flood stage from downtown Baton Rouge

p. 4 Riverwalk, New Orleans

p. 6 A view from the crescent in the river at sunrise, New Orleans

p. 8 Lake Fausse Pointe State Park, near Morgan City, Louisiana

p. 10 Cypress tree in Lake Fausse

p. 12 Lake Fausse on a foggy morning

p. 14 Rosetta spoonbill in the Atchafalaya Basin

p. 15 Lake Fausse at sunset. The photograph was taken at the time the cane fields were burning, creating the red sky.

p. 16 Water lily in Lake Martin. The photograph was taken in June during a kayak trip with my daughters to celebrate my birthday.

p. 18 Lake Martin, near Breaux Bridge

p. 20 Lake Fausse on an early morning kayak trip

p. 22 City Park Lake in Baton Rouge on a foggy morning

p. 24 University Lake at sunset

p. 26 University Lake in the fall

p. 28 City Park, Baton Rouge

22

24

26

28

29

29

30

31

32

34

36

38

39

40

42

44

46

47

48

50

52

54

56

58

59

60

62

64

66

68

70

72

74

76

77

78

80

82

84

84

85

86

88

90

92

94

96

98

Also by Randy P. Roussel

Baton Rouge: Views along the Meander

Meandering Through the Red Stick Region

Heavy Air and Sweet Cane: My Father, Family, and Three Hundred Years along the Mississippi

Privately published

Printed in South Korea by Four Colour Print Group, Louisville, Kentucky

The paper used in this publication meets the minimum requirements of the American National Standard for Information Sciences—Permanece of Paper for Printed Library Materials. ANSI Z93.48-1992

LCCN: 2019905786

ISBN: 978-0-9903675-3-6

First Edition

For further information about a photograph or for permission to use, please contact Randy P. Roussel at rousselkids@cox.net. Photographs contained in this book are available at https:// Randy-Roussel.smugmug.com.

PBC

Design by Pratt Brothers Composition